中文・English・日本語・Español

Jing Si Aphorisms

靜思語 【典藏版】

Shih Cheng Yen

釋證嚴 著

in Chinese, English, Japanese and Spanish

Buddhist Tzu Chi Foundation 佛教慈濟基金會
1100 S. Valley Center Ave. San Dimas, CA 91773
909.447.7799 | www.us.tzuchi.org
http://jingsi.us.tzuchi.org

做中學　學中覺

While working, learn;
while learning, awaken
to the many truths of life.

時間可以造就人格，
可以成就事業，
也可以儲積功德。

*Over time, we can
build great character,
achieve great success,
and cultivate great virtue.*

時間を用いて、人格を形成することも
事業を成就させることも、
また功徳を積むこともできる。

*Con el tiempo podemos
forjar un gran carácter,
alcanzar gran éxito
y cultivar una gran virtud.*

用智慧探討人生真義，
用毅力安排人生時間。

Use wisdom to
contemplate
the meaning of life.
Use resolve to organize
the time you are given.

智慧を用いて人生の真意を探究し、
気迫をもって人生のスケジュール
を決めよう。

Usa la sabiduría para meditar
sobre el significado de la vida.
Usa la determinación
para organizar el tiempo
que te es otorgado.

「前腳走，後腳放」意即：
昨天的事就讓它過去，
把心神專注於今天該做的事。

When walking,
as we step one foot forward,
we lift the other foot up.
In the same way, we should
let go of yesterday
and focus on today.

踏み出した前足が地に着いて、
後足を離さないようでは前へ進めない。
つまり、過ぎ去ったことにくよくよせず、
今日なすべき事に専心すべきである。

De la misma forma
en que apoyamos un pie
y levantamos el otro al caminar,
dejamos atrás el pasado
y nos concentramos en el presente.

未來的是妄想，過去的是雜念。
要保護此時此刻的愛心，
謹守自己當下的本分。

The future is an illusion,
the past is a memory.
Hold on to the goodness that is
in our heart at this present moment
and take care to fulfill
the duties that we have at hand.

未来のことは妄想であり、

過去のことは雑念である。

今この時の愛の心を大事にし、

今するべきことを考えてすぐに行動しよう。

El futuro es una ilusión,

el pasado es un recuerdo.

Protege el amor de este momento.

Concéntrate en tus tareas presentes.

生命無常，慧命永存；
愛心無涯，精神常在。

Transient though life may be,
one's contributions will live on;
as love knows no boundaries,
its spirit will always remain.

生命は無常であり、慧命は永遠に存在する。
愛は果てしなく、精神は常に保たれる。

La vida es efímera,
la sabiduría es eterna;
el amor en nuestros corazones
no tiene límites
y el espíritu perdurará para siempre.

最幸福的人生，
就是能寬容與悲憫
一切眾生的人生。

A person with
a generous heart
and compassion
for all beings
leads the most blessed life.

寛容と慈悲の心をもって一切衆生に接する
人生こそ最も幸せな人生である。

La persona
compasiva y generosa
con todos los seres
lleva la vida más dichosa.

不辭勞苦的付出，
便是「慈悲」。

To willingly
undergo hardship
for the sake of helping others
is compassion.

労苦を厭わない奉仕は「慈悲」である。

El someterse voluntariamente
a dificultades por el bienestar
de los demás es compasión.

即使已達智慧圓融，
更應含蓄謙虛，
像稻穗一樣，
米粒愈飽滿垂得愈低。

Those who have great wisdom
must all the more be humble and unassuming,
just like the rice stalk that bows
under the weight of ripe grain.

たとえ円融無碍の智慧に達しても、
実れば実るほど垂れ下がる稲穂ように、
さらに含蓄と謙虚さがなくてはならない。

Hasta la persona más sabia
debe ser humilde y sin pretensiones,
como el tallo de arroz
que se inclina
bajo el peso
del grano maduro.

唯有尊重自己的人，
才能勇於縮小自己。

Only those
who respect themselves
have the courage
to be humble.

己を尊重する人こそ
勇んで自分を縮めることができる。

Sólo aquellos
que se respetan a sí mismos
tienen el valor
de ser humildes.

縮小自己，要能縮到對方的眼睛裡，
還要能嵌在對方的心頭上。

To be humble
is to shrink our ego
until we are small enough
to enter another's eyes
and reside in
their heart and mind.

相手の目の中、耳の中に入れるほどに
己を縮小すれば、相手を傷つけず、
また相手の心の中まで入り込むことができる。

Ser humilde
es disminuir nuestro ego
lo suficiente como para penetrar
a través de los ojos de los demás,
y alojarnos en sus corazones
y en sus mentes.

看淡自己是般若，
看重自己是執著。

To regard ourself lightly
is prajna (wisdom).
To regard ourself highly
is attachment.

淡白な己であれば般若であり、
己を重んじるのは執着である。

El vernos a nosotros mismos con modestia
es Prajna (sabiduría).
El considerarnos altamente
es aferrarse a uno mismo.

不能低頭的人，
是因為一再回顧過去的成就。

People who are
preoccupied
with past achievements
cannot humble themselves.

いつまでも過去の功績にこだわっていると、
頭を低くすることができない。

Las personas
que se preocupan constantemente
en logros pasados
no saben ser humildes.

人都是在原諒自己的
那一分鐘開始懈怠。

We start to slacken
the minute we find excuses
for ourselves.

自分自身を許したその時から、
その人は怠惰になってゆく。

Comenzamos a aflojar
apenas encontramos una excusa.

勇於承擔，
是一分動人的力量；
勇於承擔錯誤，
則是一種高尚的品格。

To shoulder a burden
is an inspiring force.
To admit a mistake
is a noble virtue.

率先していろんなことを担って行く人は
敬服に値する。
また率直に自分の過ちを認める人は、
気高い品格の持ち主である。

El llevar una carga
es una fuerza inspiradora,
el admitir un error
es una noble virtud.

大錯誤容易反省，
小習氣不易去除。

*It is easy to reflect on
major mistakes,
and hard to eliminate
small bad habits.*

大きな過ちを犯した時は、
容易に反省をするものだが、
些細な良くない習慣はなかなか改められない。

Es fácil reflexionar
sobre los grandes errores
pero difícil eliminar
las pequeñas malas costumbres.

懺悔則清淨，
清淨則能去除煩惱。

Repentance
purifies the mind;
a pure mind
can readily
sweep away afflictions.

懺悔して心を清めれば
煩悩は取り除くことができる。

El arrepentimiento
purifica la mente;
una mente pura
elimina fácilmente
las preocupaciones.

人最難看見的，
就是自己。

The hardest thing
for people to see
is themselves.

一番見極め難いのは自分自身である。

El mirar con claridad
hacia dentro
de uno mismo
es lo más difícil
para los seres humanos.

036

信心、毅力、勇氣三者具備，
天下沒有做不成的事。

Nothing is impossible
with confidence,
perseverance,
and courage.

信念、毅力、勇気の三つが揃えば、
この世にできないことはない。

Con fe,
perseverancia
y valor, no hay nada
que no podamos realizar.

要以理來轉事，
不是拿事來轉理。

We must carry out our tasks
according to principles,
and not let our principles
be compromised by our tasks.

大切なのは「理」でもって
「事」を扱うことで、「事」でもって
「理」を扱うものではない。

Debemos llevar a cabo nuestras tareas
de acuerdo a nuestros principios
y no dejar que nuestros principios
se vean comprometidos por nuestras tareas.

凡事要守好自己的原則，
不要牽強應酬；
常去應酬，
往往度不到對方，
反而會被拖下水。

Abide by your principles in everything you do.
Never do things just to satisfy others.
For rather than satifisfying them,
you may get in over your head.

何事にも自分の原則を守ることが大切だ。
無理してまで招待に応じることはない。
無理な付き合いを重ねていたら、
往々にして相手を感化するよりも
相手に丸め込まれてしまいやすい。

Rígete por tus principios
en todo lo que hagas.
Nunca actúes simplemente
para complacer a los demás,
porque en vez de ayudarlos,
te verás envuelto
en una situación difícil.

好事，需要你、我、他共同來成就。
所以，不要有你、我、他的成見。

Good actions require
everyone's cooperation.
So let's not cling to personal biases.

良い事はみんなで力を合わせて
成就しなければならない。
よって、それぞれの
先入観は禁物である。

Las buenas acciones
requieren la cooperación de todos.
Deja a un lado
los prejuicios personales.

處理事情，
感情要蘊藏在理智中；
與人相處，
則要把感情表現在理智上。

In handling matters,
let your mind
influence your heart.
In dealing with people,
let your heart
influence your mind.

事を処理する際、
感情は理知の中にしまっておき、
人と触れ合う時は
感情を理知の上に表す。

Cuando estés trabajando,
permite que tu corazón
se deje influir por tu mente.
Cuando trates con la gente,
permite que tu mente
se deje influir por tu corazón.

整體的美，
在於個體的修養。

*The beauty of a group
lies in the refinement
of its individuals.*

全体の美は、個人の修養により現れる。

La belleza de un grupo
está en el
refinamiento
de los individuos.

一個人的修養、氣質，
均在行、住、坐、臥四威儀中
自然地顯露出來。

A refined disposition
is naturally expressed
in the way a person
walks, lives, sits,
and sleeps.

修養、気質というものは、
日常の行住坐臥の行儀作法の中に
自然に現れる。

Una actitud refinada
se expresa
naturalmente en la forma
en que una persona
camina, vive,
se sienta y duerme.

欣賞他人，
即是莊嚴自己。

Because seeing virtue in others
is in itself a virtue,
in appreciating others,
we in fact dignify ourselves.

他人を称賛することは、
自分自身を荘厳にすることになる。

El apreciar a los demás
es dignificarnos.

世間的物資本來是為人所用，
但不知足者因欠缺智慧，
竟淪為「被物所用」。

Material objects were meant to be
tools for us to use.
Yet, lacking wisdom,
we are perpetually discontent,
and we thus become
enslaved by material objects.

世の中の物は本来人間に
使われるものであるが、
足るを知ることができない人は
智慧に乏しいため
「物に使われる」羽目になる。

Las cosas materiales
se han hecho para usarse;
aún así,
las personas se vuelven
disconformes y esclavas de ellas
cuando no tienen sabiduría.

人生有求即多苦！
如果只是一味地要求他人，
會為自己招來無窮的痛苦。

How bitter life is
when we have desires!
Our demands on others
bring endless misery.

人生において求めることがあると苦労する。
ひたすら人に求めて止まないなら
限りない苦痛を招くことになる。

¡Cuán amarga es la vida
cuando engendramos deseos!
Nuestras exigencias hacia el prójimo
nos traen infinitas penas.

人生若能減低欲望，
生活上便沒有什麼值得計較！

If we can
reduce our desires,
there is nothing
really worth
getting upset about.

欲望を減らせば日常生活において
何も争うほどのことはない。

Si logramos
disminuir nuestros deseos,
no hay nada
por lo que realmente
valga la pena enfadarse.

知足的人，心量開闊；
心量開闊，對人對事就不會計較。

One who is content
is immensely broadhearted.
A broadhearted person
will not be
in dispute with others
over any matter.

足るを知る人は度量が広い。
度量が広いので人に対しても
事に対しても争わない。

Una persona satisfecha
tiene un gran corazón.
La persona con un gran corazón
no se pelea con nadie
por ningún motivo.

人要知福、惜福、再造福。

Know your blessings,
cherish them and sow more blessings.

人は福を知り、福を惜しみ、
さらに福を造るべきである。

Date cuenta que estás bendito
y aprecia estas bendiciones;
luego, sigue cultivando
más bendiciones.

世間的海可以填平，
但是小小一個嘴巴，
卻永遠填不滿。

The ocean can be filled,
yet the tiny mouth
of a human being
can never be filled.

海を埋めてしまうことはできても、
人間の小さな口はいくら埋めても
満ちることがない。

El océano se puede llenar;
sin embargo,
la boca diminuta
de un ser humano
nunca se llenaría.

學佛的第一步是要少欲知足，
使心靈安住，智慧增長。

The first step on the path of Buddhism
is to lessen our desires and be satisfied with
what we have.
Then our minds will relax and we will begin
to gain wisdom.

仏に学ぶ第一歩は「欲少なく、
足るを知ること」によって
心を落ち着かせ、
智慧を増やすことである。

El primer paso
para aprender budismo
es disminuir nuestros deseos
y estar satisfechos con lo que tenemos;
de esta manera,
con nuestras mentes en calma,
empezaremos a ganar sabiduría.

以愛待人、以慈對人，
則不惹人怨，亦能結好緣。

When we treat others
with loving-kindness,
we will not stir up ill feelings,
and we will be able to
form good relationships with others.

慈愛をもって人と接することができれば
人に恨まれることはなく、
良いつながりをもつことができる。

Si tratamos a otros
con amor y compasión,
no crearemos malos sentimientos.
Sin crear malos sentimientos,
podremos entablar
buenas relaciones con los demás.

菩薩不是土塑木刻的形象，
真正的菩薩能做事、能說話、能吃飯，
能尋聲救苦隨處現身。

Bodhisattvas are not
idols made of wood;
real Bodhisattvas are people
who eat, talk, work,
and relieve suffering
in times of need.

菩薩とは土で造ったり
木で彫ったりした造形ではない。
真の菩薩は仕事ができ、言葉が話せ、
ご飯が食べられ、救いを求める声を聞くと
随所に姿を現す。

Los Bodhisattvas
no son estatuas de madera,
sino, personas que comen,
hablan, trabajan
y alivian el sufrimiento de otros
en tiempos de necesidad.

人人本具菩薩心，
也具有和菩薩同等的精神與力量。

Everyone has
a Buddha nature,
and a Bodhisattva's
strength and spirit.

人はもともと菩薩の心をもっており、
また菩薩と同じような精神と
力量を備えている。

Todos tenemos
la esencia del Buda,
y la fortaleza y el espíritu
de un Bodhisattva.

佛法很簡單，
只要去除貪、瞋、癡三毒，
就可以明心見性。

Dharma is very simple:
eliminate greed, malice,
and ignorance,
and you will discover
your own true nature.

仏法は至って簡単で、貪、瞋、痴を
除きさえすれば悟ることができるのである。

El Dharma es muy sencillo,
si eliminas la avaricia,
la malicia y la ignorancia,
descubrirás tu propia
verdadera naturaleza.

直心即道場。

Be faithful and honest
from deep inside,
this is the essence
of spiritual cultivation.

直心すなわち道場

Ten fe y sé honesto de corazón,
estas son la esencias
de la cultivación espiritual.

教法不必聽太多，
若能身體力行，
簡單的一句，
就能啓發真正的善根。

There is no need to learn
many teachings.
If we can put one simple
verse into practice,
we can awaken
our true nature of goodness.

あれこれと教えを多く聞くまでもない。
実践さえすれば、簡単な一言が即ち真法となり
真の善根を啓發することになる。

No hay necesidad
de aprender muchas enseñanzas.
Si somos capaces
de poner un simple verso en práctica,
podremos despertar
la bondad innata
que hay en nosotros.

每天都是生命中的一張白紙，
每一個人、每一件事
都是一篇生動的文章。

Every single day
is like a blank page of our life.
Every person we meet,
every event we participate in
is a lively essay.

毎日が生命における一枚の白紙の
ようなものであり、一人一人のどんな出来事でも
一篇の生き生きとした文章に
綴ることができる。

Cada día de nuestra vida
es como una página nueva.
Cada persona que conocemos
y cada acontecimiento
en que participamos
son una redacción animada.

人一生的行為，
不管是善是惡，
皆由時間所累積。

The behavior of a person
during his lifetime,
be it good or evil,
is accumulated over time.

一生の行爲は善にしろ悪にしろ、
ことごとく時間によつて積み重ねられる。

El comportamiento de una persona
en el transcurso de su vida,
sea bueno o malo,
se acumula con el tiempo.

每天無所事事，
是人生的消費者；
積極付出，
才是人生的創造者。

Doing nothing
and idling time away
consumes life.
Giving to others
with total dedication
creates life.

毎日ぶらぶらしている人は
ただ人生の消費者であり、
積極的に奉仕する人こそが
人生の創造者なのである。

La vide se desgasta
si derrochamos el tiempo
y no hacemos nada.
El entregarse a otros
con total dedicación
llena nuestras vidas.

什麼都沒做，就是空過的人生；
若能不斷付出利益人群，
就是大好的人生。

If we don't do something meaningful,
our life will pass by in vain.
But if we work unceasingly
for the betterment of mankind,
ours will be a beautiful life.

何もしないのは人生を無駄に
費やすことになり、
世に益する事を絶えず実行すれば
最高の人生となる。

La vida no tiene sentido
si pasamos los días
sin hacer nada.
La vida es maravillosa
si se trabaja sin descanso
por el bienestar
de la humanidad.

為人處事要小心、細心，
但不要「小心眼」！

Be careful and mindful
when dealing with others,
but do not be
narrow-minded.

何をするにも細やかな注意が必要だが、
心が狭くならないように。

No actúes
con la mente cerrada
al tratar con los demás,
sé cuidadoso y considerado.

雙手健全卻不肯做事的人，
等於是沒有手的人。

To have two good hands
and refuse to work
is no different than
having no hands at all.

健全な両手がありながら働こうとしない人は
手がないのと同じである。

Tener dos manos útiles
y rehusar a trabajar
es lo mismo
que no tener ninguna mano.

做人固然不應將自我看得太重，
但也不要自輕己靈。

Do not think too highly
of yourself,
and yet,
never underestimate
your ability.

人は自分自身をあまり重く
見てはならないが、
だからと言って己を軽んじるのではない。

No te sobreestimes,
pero tampoco subestimes
tu propia habilidad.

要平安，得先心安；
要心安，須先得理；
理得心安，即闔家平安。

To live in peace, we must have inner peace.
To have inner peace, we
must have a clear conscience.
When our conscience is
clear and our mind at peace,
we bring peace and bliss
to those around us.

平安でありたければ先ず心を安らかに、
心安らかにありたければ
先ず道理をわきまえることだ。
道理をわきまえ心安らかになれば、
みんなが平安となれる。

Para vivir en paz,
debemos tener paz interna.
Para tener paz interna,
debemos tener conciencia clara.
Cuando nuestra conciencia está clara
y nuestra mente en paz, traemos paz
y bendición a quienes nos rodean.

難行能行，難捨能捨，難為能為，
才能昇華自我的人格。

Continue even when it is hard to go on,
release even when it is hard to let go,
endure even when it is hard to bear,
this is how we build our character.

行き難きを行き、捨て難きを捨ててこそ、
自己の人格を昇華させることができる。

Continúa
aunque sea difícil,
deja ir
aunque sea difícil dejarlo,
aguanta aunque sea difícil aguantarlo,
así es como forjarás tu carácter.

口說好話，心想好意，
身行好事，腳走好路。

Speak kind words,
think good thoughts,
do good deeds,
and walk the right path.

良い言葉を口にし、
善良な心で、
善行をなそう。

Utiliza buenas palabras,
ten buenos pensamientos,
haz buenas obras
y camina por el sendero correcto.

轉一個角度來看世界，
世界無限寬大；
換一種立場來待人處事，
人事無不輕安。

When you view the world
from a different perspective,
the world becomes vast and wide.
Try shifting your perspective
in everything you do,
and all will be light and easy.

物事の見方を変えて見ると、
世界は無限に広く大きく感じる。
事に臨んだ時、ちょっと立場を変えて見ると、
深刻に思えた事も何でもないことに
思えてくるものだ。

Mira al mundo
con otra perspectiva,
el mundo es vasto y amplio.
Todo será más fácil
si utilizamos diferentes puntos de vista
al tratar con los demás.

做事，
一定要秉持「誠」與「正」的原則；
而待人，
則要用「寬」與「柔」的態度。

Be honest and truthful
in everything you do.
Be gentle and forgiving
in your relationships
with others.

事にあたる時は必ず「誠」と「正」の
原則に則り、
人に対しては「寛」と「柔」の
態度で接しよう。

Sé honesto y sincero
en todo lo que hagas.
Sé gentil y perdona
a los demás en tus relaciones.

人生因為有責任而踏實，
逃避責任就是虛度人生。

Life becomes meaningful
when we shoulder
responsibilities.
Avoiding responsibilities
makes our life empty.

責任感があってこそ人生は着実となる。
責任逃れしようものなら
虚しい人生になってしまう。

La vida tiene significado
cuando asumimos responsabilidades.
El evitar responsabilidades
hace que nuestra vida
se vuelva vacía.

不要因貪求清閒，
而希求減輕責任；
應該增強自己的力量，
擔當更重大的責任。

Do not ask for less responsibility
to be free and relaxed —
ask for more strength.

安逸を貪るため責任の軽減を
求めてはならない。
自分の力を強めて、
さらに重大な責任を担うべきである。

No pidas
menos responsabilidades
para sentirte
libre y relajado,
sino, pide más fortaleza.

與其擔心社會現狀，
不如化作信心，
並付出一分愛心。

Rather than worry about
the condition of our society,
why not replace it
with confidence and with dedication
to contribute with loving-kindness?

社會の現状を心配するより、
信じる心に転じて「愛」を
供出することである。

En vez de preocuparte
por la situación de nuestra sociedad,
¿ Por qué no reemplazar esta preocupación
con firmeza y dedicación
para así contribuir con amor?

即使自己只是一根小螺絲釘，
也要注意有沒有鎖上、鎖緊，
以便充分發揮功能。

Even the tiniest bolt
must be screwed on tightly
in order to perform its best.

たとえ自分はただ一本の小さな
ネジでしかなくても、
固く締まっているかどうか注意して、
充分に機能を発揮せねばならない。

Hasta las tuercas más pequeñas
tienen que ser bien ajustadas
para alcanzar
el óptimo funcionamiento.

碰到逆境時，
應心生感激，
這是可遇不可求啊！

In the face of adversity,
be grateful,
for such opportunities
do not come by easily.

逆境の中に身を置いた時、
ありがたいチャンスだと
感謝すべきである。

Sé agradecido
ante la adversidad;
oportunidades como estas
no se presentan fácilmente.

逆境、是非來臨，
心中要持一「寬」字。

When conflict and
adversity arise,
always preserve
a spacious heart.

「寛」という一字を持して
「逆境」「是非」に対処しよう。

Mantén siempre
un corazón magnánimo
aún cuando surgen
el conflicto y la adversidad.

要原諒一個無心傷害人的人，
不能做一個輕易就被別人傷害的人。

Forgive those
who unintentionally hurt us.
Do not be someone
who is easily hurt by others.

何気なく言つたことで
他人を傷つけてしまうような人を
咎のずに許してあげよう。
たやすく他人に傷つけられるような
人になってはいけない。

Perdona a aquellas personas
que nos lastiman sin querer.
No seas alguien
a quien otros puedan
lastimar con facilidad.

人在平安的時候，很容易迷失自己。
偶爾有小挫折或坎坷，
反而能喚醒良知、長養善根。

When life is safe and smooth,
we can easily lose our direction.
Yet even a small setback or misfortune
can awaken our conscience,
and nurture the seeds of kindness.

人は無事でいると己を見失いがちである。

たまに小さな挫折や

順調にいかないことでもあれば、

かえって良知を呼び覚まし、

善根を養うことができる。

〈注〉良知：人の生まれながらにしてそなえた知能。

Es fácil perderse

cuando uno siente

que la vida es segura y tranquila.

Sin embargo,

un pequeño tropezón o desgracia ocacional,

puede despertar nuestra conciencia

y sembrar las semillas de bondad.

人應該相信自己，
但是不可執著。

Believe in yourself,
but do not be attached
to your own point of view.

自分を信じるべきではあるが、
過信して執着してはならない。

Cree en tí mismo,
pero no te aferres sólo
a tu propio punto de vista.

無信與迷信二者，
寧願「無信」也不要「迷信」；
信必須智信。

Atheism
is better than
superstition.
Faith must be guided
by wisdom.

信じないのと迷信とどちらを選ぶかというと、

迷信よりは信じないほうがいい。

信ずるなら智慧ある信心であるべきで、

ありもしないことを信じるべきではない。

El ateísmo es preferible

a la superstición.

La fe debe ser guiada

por la sabiduría.

智信者深體佛法之精神，
迷信者曲解宗教之美意。

A wise believer understands
the essence of Buddhism.
Those who are
superstitious misinterpret
the virtue of religion.

智慧ある信者は仏法の精神を深く
体得できるが、迷信に傾く人は
宗教の真意を曲解する。

Aquel que cree y tiene sabiduría
entiende la esencia del Budismo.
Aquellos que son supersticiosos
malinterpretan la virtud de la religión.

人有正確的信仰，
在人生旅途走的路就不會有差錯。

When one has correct faith,
one will not go wrong
on the journey of life.

正しい信仰があれば、
人生の旅をさして誤ることはない。

Cuando tienes
una fe correcta,
no desviarás
en el camino de la vida.

迷信就會疑心生暗鬼、問神卜卦，
取信於籤詩、筊杯，
而無法真正深入教理。

False understanding
leads to superstition,
the search for answers from
psychics and soothsayers; in this way,
we cannot realize the ultimate truth
of the teachings.

迷信は疑心暗鬼を生み、
占いを信じて神頼みするばかりで、
教理を本当に深く体得できない。

Las falsas interpretaciones
llevan a la superstición,
a la búsqueda de respuestas
por parte de videntes y psíquicos.
De esta forma, no podemos darnos
cuenta de la verdad absoluta
de las enseñanzas.

「修」是修心養性，
「行」是端正行為。

*The process
of spiritual cultivation
is to nurture virtue
and rectify conduct
and behavior.*

「修」とは、心を修め気質を養うことで、
「行」とは、正しい行いのことである。

El proceso
de la cultivación espiritual
consiste en nutrir la virtud
y rectificar la conducta
y el comportamiento.

同道，是指同修間若有錯誤的行為，
可彼此更正、相互惕勵。

To walk the same path
of spiritual cultivation means
practitioners unite to
inspire each other
and reflect on weaknesses
in behavior and conduct.

同道とは、
もし修行の仲間の内に誤った行爲があれば、
互いに指摘し、
戒め合うことを指す。

El caminar la misma senda
de la cultivación espiritual
significa que los practicantes
se unen para inspirarse mutuamente
y reflexionar sobre la debilidad
del comportamiento y la conducta.

人既然生在世間，
就不能離開眾緣，
修行也不能離群隱世。

Born into this world,
we are always with people;
hence spiritual cultivation
cannot be achieved in isolation.

人としてこの世に生を受けたからには、
衆生との縁を離れることはできず、
修行するにも群衆を離れ、
隠遁して行うことはできない。

133

El haber nacido en este mundo
nos hace estar siempre rodeados de gente.
Es así como la cultivación espiritual
no puede ocurrir en aislamiento.

134

一切言行舉止能精神統一，
　心念一致，就是禪定。

When our spirit and actions
are in harmony;
when our heart and thoughts
are in accord,
that is deep meditation.

言行挙止の一切において、
精神を統一し、心念を一致させることが
「禅定」である。

Cuando nuestro espíritu y acciones están
en armonía
y cuando nuestro corazón y pensamientos
están de acuerdo,
eso es meditación profunda.

「戒」是不起心動念；
「定」是臨危不亂；
「慧」能運心轉境。

Precepts allow our mind to be free from disturbance.

Equanimity allows us to be calm under adversity.

Wisdom allows us to take control of our mind and change our destiny.

戒：心静かに本分を守り、
　　あらゆる貪りの念を断つ。
定：どんなに困った時でも、
　　志操を堅持し、
　　危機に臨んでも乱れない。
慧：心を理想の境地に導く。

Los preceptos permiten que nuestra mente
esté libre de perturbaciones.
El estar libre de perturbaciones
nos permite mantener
la calma ante el peligro.
La sabiduría nos permite tener
control de la mente
y cambiar nuestro destino.

對人有疑心，就無法愛人；
對人有疑念，就無法原諒人；
對人有疑惑，就無法相信人。

We cannot love when filled with suspicion.
We cannot trust when filled with doubts.
We cannot forgive when unwilling to believe.

人に対して疑心があれば、
人を愛することはできない。
人に対して疑念があれば、
人を許すことはできない。
人に対して疑惑があれば、
人を信じることはできない。

139

No podemos amar
cuando estamos llenos de sospechas.
No podemos perdonar
cuando estamos llenos de dudas.
No podemos confiar
cuando no estamos dispuestos a creer.

多一分對他人的疑慮，
就少一分對自己的信心。

The more mistrust we feel,
the less confidence we have.

他人をそれだけ疑えば、
自分もそれだけ自信を失う。

Cuanto más desconfianza tengamos,
menos confianza tenemos.

一個真正成功的人，
必須人人都能容得下你，
你也能容納每一個人。

A truly successful person
is accepted by everyone
and accepts everyone.

真の成功者は誰からも受け入れられ、
また、誰をも受け入れられる人で
なければならない。

Una persona verdaderamente exitosa
es aceptada por todos
y acepta a todos.

如何達到生死自在的境界？
唯有靠平常多培養「喜捨」之心，
方達提得起、放得下之境界。

How can we be free from the suffering of
birth and death?
Only when we nurture our heart with joy
and unselfish
giving can we truly release
our attachments.

どうすれば生死自在の境地に
達することができるか。
それは「捨てることのできる心を培う」
という日頃の心掛けに頼るしかない。
それでこそ「放下できる」境地に達せる。

Cómo podemos estar libres
del sufrimiento de la vida y de la muerte?
Solamente cuando dejamos ir
nuestras ataduras
y alimentamos nuestros
corazones con alegría
y la entrega desinteresada,
así podemos dejar de tenacear.

捨去眼前的煩惱，
才能當下擁有慈悲的法喜。

Let go of all worries,
only then will you experience
the happiness of a
compassionate heart.

目の前の煩悩を捨ててこそ、
ただちに慈悲の法悦に浴することができる。

Deja ir las preocupaciones;
sólo así apreciarás la alegría
de un corazón compasivo.

付出勞力又歡喜，
便叫做「喜捨」。

To give with joy
is to help others
with a happy mood.

労力で喜んで奉仕するのを「喜捨」という。

El dar con alegría es
ayudar a otros con felicidad.

有人點燈求光明，
其實真正的光明在我們心裡。

Many seek illumination
by lighting up a lamp,
when the true light
is within.

光明なる前途を祈願して
仏前に灯を点す人がいる。
だが、真の光明は自分の心の中にある。

Muchos buscan la iluminación
encendiendo una lámpara,
pero la verdadera luz
está dentro de uno mismo.

人的心地就像一畝田，
若沒有播下好的種子，
也長不出好的果實來。

Our mind is like a garden;
if no good seeds are sown,
nothing good
will grow from it.

人の心は田んぼと同じで、
良い種を蒔かなければ
よい実を結ぶことはできない。

Nuestra mente
es como un jardín;
si no sembramos
buenas semillas,
nada bueno crecerá.

天堂和地獄，
都是由心和行為所造作。

Our thoughts
and actions create
our destiny of
heaven or hell.

天国も地獄も心と行爲によって造られる。

Nuestros pensamientos
y acciones
crean nuestro destino
en el cielo o en el infierno.

三心二意無定性，
四處徘徊不專精，
儘管條條道路通長安，
卻永遠無法到達終點！

Even if every road led to Rome,
when our mind is indecisive,
constantly wandering,
and unable to concentrate,
we will never make it
to our destination.

優柔不断で、物事に専心することなく
うろつき回っていたら、
目的地に通ずる道が何本あっても、
永遠に終点へはたどり着けない。

Incluso si todos los caminos
conducen a Roma,
una mente indecisa
que deambula e
incapaz de concentrarse,
nunca será capaz
de llegar a su destino.

要用心，
不要操心、煩心。

When doing something,
instead of worrying
or being vexed about it,
we should just be mindful.

やさしく心を配ろう。

心を労することなく、煩わすことなく。

Debes estar atento,

no preocupado ni perturbado.

人的觀念不正，
就不能正業；
觀念如果偏差，
所做的事也會錯誤。

If our view is incorrect,
our actions will not be right;
if our thinking is biased,
everything we do will be wrong.

正しい観念を持たなければ、
正業を行うことは難しい。
観念に偏りがあれば、
行いに誤りが生じ易くなる。

Si nuestro punto de vista
es incorrecto, nuestras acciones
tampoco serán correctas;
si nuestra forma de pensar
está prejuiciada, todo lo que hacemos
será incorrecto.

人要學習經得起周圍人事的
磨練而心不動搖，
並學習在動中保持心的寧靜。

Learn to remain undisturbed
in the tumult of people and events.
Remain at peace inside yourself even when
busy and occupied.

人間は、周囲の「人」や「事」の練磨の
中で不動の心を保てるよう、
「動」の中で心の平静さを
保つことができるよう、修行を積むべきである。

*Debemos aprender a mantener la
calma entre el tumulto de las personas
y los acontecimientos,
a mantener la paz interior,
incluso cuando estamos muy ocupados.*

有智慧的人能捨，
能「捨」就能「得」，
得到無限的快樂。

A wise person is able to let go.
To let go is actually to receive,
to receive boundless happiness.

智慧のある人は捨て切ることができるから、
「捨てて」この上ない喜びを
「得る」ことができる。

Una persona sabia es una persona
capaz de no apegarse a nada.
El no apegarse a nada es recibir,
recibir felicidad infinita.

智慧是從人與事之間磨練出來的，
若逃避現實，離開人與事，
便無從產生智慧。

Spiritual wisdom is cultivated in the
interplay of people, objects, and events.
To escape from reality,
to keep away from people and events,
provides no means to nurture wisdom.

智慧は人と事とのかかわり合いによって
磨き出される。
現実から逃避し、人と事から
遠ざかっていては、
智慧は到底育たない。

La sabiduría espiritual
se cultiva mediante la interacción
de las personas,
los objetos y los acontecimientos.
Escaparse de la realidad, alejarse de las
personas y de los acontecimientos no
nos ofrece medios para
enriquecer nuestra sabiduría.

有些人常常起煩惱——
因為別人一句無心的話，
他卻有意的接受。

People often feel upset
because they take careless remarks
too seriously.

話し手はそのつもりでないのに、
聞き手が独り合点して煩悩を
起こすことがままある。

Las personas
se sienten a menudo enojadas
porque toman muy en serio comentarios,
dichos a la ligera.

如果有所付出就想有所回報，
將會招來煩惱。

Giving with
an expectation for return
brings misery.

見返りを求める奉仕は煩悩の元となる。

El dar con expectativa
de recibir algo a cambio
sólo trae miseria.

「貪」不但帶來痛苦，
也使人墮落。

172

Craving
not only brings misery,
but also leads the way to moral ruin.

「貪り」は苦痛をもたらすばかりでなく、
人を堕落させる。

La codicia
no sólo trae miseria,
sino que también
puede llevarnos a la ruina.

人生多欲為苦——
人常被「欲」所牽引造業。

Suffering is caused by
man's endless desire,
which draws people to do evil
and create bad karma.

欲が多ければ苦しむ。
人はとかく欲に引きずられて、
悪業を造る。

Los seres humanos
sufren porque tienen
deseos constantemente.
Estos deseos los conducen
a hacer algo malo
y crear mal karma.

煩惱就像一條毒蛇睡在人的心中，
一觸動它，蛇就會咬人。

Worry is a poisonous snake
that sleeps in the mind;
the moment you disturb it,
the snake will bite you.

煩悩はあたかも一匹の毒蛇が人の心の中に
眠っているようなもので、
いったん毒蛇に触れたらかみついてくる。

Las preocupaciones
son como serpientes venenosas
que duermen en la mente;
en el momento que las molestes,
te morderán.

人生有煩惱，
皆源貪、瞋、癡三毒所引起。

All worries in life flow
from three poisons:
greed, malice and ignorance.

人生に煩悩があるのは人の心に
三毒－貪、瞋、痴があるためである。

En la vida,
todas las preocupaciones derivan de
tres fuentes venenosas:
la codicia, la malicia y la ignorancia.

能為人服務比被人服務有福。

It is more of a blessing
to serve others than to be served.

ひとに奉仕することができる人は、
奉仕される人よりも福がある。

Es mayor bendición servir a otros
que ser servido.

多原諒人一次，
就多造一次福；
把量放大，福就大。

Each time we forgive others,
we are, in fact, sowing blessings.
The more magnanimity we show,
the more blessings we enjoy.

今一度人を許せば、
今一度福をつくったことになる。
度量を広く持てば福も大きくなる。

Perdonar una vez
es ser bendecido una vez.
Cuanto más perdonemos,
más seremos bendecidos.

自造福田，自得福緣。

Those who sow
the seeds of blessings
shall harvest plentiful blessings.

自ら福田をたがやせば、
自ずと福縁（幸せをもたらす縁）を得る。

Aquellos que siembran
las semillas de la bendición cosecharán
una multitud de bendiciones.

人與人相處，都是以聲色互相對待。
講話是聲，態度是色，
與人講話要輕言細語，
態度要微笑寬柔。

The expressions on our face and the tone of
our voice all communicate to others.
So smile and speak softly;
preserve a gentle attitude.

人と人との交流は、
すべて「声色」をもって伝え合うもの。
「声」とは話すことで、
「色」とは態度だ。
それゆえ対話はふんわりと優しい口調で、
微笑みを湛えた丁寧な態度にしたいもの。

Nos comunicamos con los demás
por medio de nuestras
expresiones del rostro y
del tono de nuestra voz.
Sonríe y habla con voz suave,
mantén una actitud apacible.

聽話、說話要完整，
不要只揀前一句、後一句，
合起來剛好尖尖地刺進人心。

Be clear and complete
when you talk and listen.
Do not pick one sentence here,
and one sentence there;
or you may by accident
intensely hurt someone.

話を聞くのも話すのも、完全を期すことだ。
自分の都合によって前のほうから一語、
後ろのほうから一語と勝手に選んで、
それを繋いでみると人を傷つけるような
とげとげしい話になってしまうということに
ならないように。

Sé claro y completo
cuando estés escuchando o hablando.
No tomes una frase por aquí
y otra por allá, o puede ser que
involuntariamente lastimes
mucho a alguien.

對人要寬心，
講話要細心。

Be forgiving towards others.
Be discreet in your speech.

他人には寛容に、
話す時は細心の注意をはらって。

Olvida las ofensas
de otras personas.
Sé discreto en tus conversaciones.

要做個受人歡迎和被愛的人，
必須先照顧好自我的聲和色。

*To win the hearts of others and always
be welcomed, we must be cautious of
our tone of voice and facial expression.*

歓迎され愛される人になるには、
先ず自分の声音と身振りに
気をつけるべきである。

Para ganarse el corazón de los demás y
ser siempre bienvenidos,
debemos ser cautelosos con
nuestro tono de voz y con
nuestras expresiones faciales.

只要緣深，不怕緣來得遲；
只要找到路，就不怕路遙遠。

It is never too late for a
deep-rooted affinity to blossom.
Do not worry over
a distant journey as long as
one finds the way.

縁さえ深ければ、
それが遅れようとも気にすることはない。
道さえ見つければ、
その道がいかに遠くても恐れることはない。

Siempre que una afinidad sea profunda,
no temas que tarde en llegar.
Del mismo modo, no temas que
una trayectoria sea larga,
siempre que hayas encontrado el camino.

有願放在心裡，
沒有身體力行，
正如耕田而不播種，
皆是空過因緣。

Making vows without taking
any action is like ploughing a field
without planting any seeds;
so, there is no harvest to reap.
This is letting opportunity pass us by.

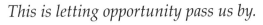

心の中に願いを持っていても、
身を持って実践しなければ、
田畑を耕しても種を
蒔かないのと同じで、機縁を無駄にしてしまう。

Hacer votos sin actuar
es como arar el campo
sin plantar ninguna semilla;
no habrá cosecha que recoger,
dejando que la oportunidad pase.

每天要感謝父母與眾生，
一生所作不要辜負父母與眾生。

Be grateful to your parents
and to all sentient beings, every day.
In everything you do,
never disappoint them.

毎日自分の両親やすべての生き物に
対して感謝することだ。
父母や衆生の恩を
無にするようなことをしてはならない。

Sé agradecido cada día
con tus padres y con todo ser viviente.
Tenlos presentes en todo lo que hagas.
Nunca los decepciones.

死是生的開頭，生是死的起點。
生生死死、死死生生，
本來就同在一個循環中。

Death is the new beginning of birth,
birth is the beginning of death.
Birth and death, living and dying,
are all part of the same cycle.

死は生の始まり、
生は死の起点なのだ。
生生死死、死死生生は
もともと同じように循環している。

La muerte es el comienzo
de un nuevo nacimiento.
El nacimiento es el comienzo de la muerte.
El nacimiento y la muerte,
el vivir y el morir son todos partes del mismo
ciclo de la existencia.

家庭不能只追求豐富的物質生活，
應著重心靈溝通，
使親子、夫妻間和諧、圓滿。

Do not just seek
a rich material life for your family.
It is more important for parent and child,
and husband and wife to communicate and
nurture harmonious and close relationships.

家庭生活において、ただ物質的な豊かさを
追求するだけではならない。
むしろ「心の通じ合い」に重きをおいて、
親子、夫婦の仲が円満にいくよう
心がけるべきである。

No persigas solamente una vida
de riquezas materiales para tu familia.
Es más importante que haya comunicación
entre padres e hijos,
así como entre esposo y esposa
y que mantengan relaciones
armoniosas y cercanas.

鳥要有巢，人要有家，
如果夫妻子女各居一方，
何來天倫之樂？

Birds have nests; people have homes.
If family members live far apart,
how can they have a happy family life?

鳥は巣を必要とし、人は家庭を必要とする。
もし夫婦や親子がそれぞれ別居していたら、
どうして一家団欒の楽しみが得られよう。

Los pájaros tienen nidos,
las personas tienen hogares.
Si los miembros de la familia
viven separados,
¿Cómo pueden tener
una vida familiar feliz?

與人相處要去除我執，
擴大心胸，客客氣氣，
互讓互愛。

You must be free of ego
when you are with others,
so expand your heart,
be courteous, cooperative, and loving.

人と付き合う時、
我執を除き寛大な心をもって、
謙虚な気持ちで互いに
譲り合い愛し合うこと。

Debes liberarte de tu ego
cuando estés con otras personas.
Abre tu corazón, sé cortés, colaborador,
amable y amoroso.

人生多病！
身體四大不調是病，
家人吵嚷不和是病，
社會動盪不安也是病。

Life is full of illness.
Disease is illness,
family dispute is illness,
social unrest is illness.

人生には病気が多い。身体の四大不調は
病気であり、家族の争いや社会の乱れも
また病気である。

〈注〉四大不調：四大は地、水、火、風のこと。
四大が調和しない時が病気である。

La vida está llena de dolencias.
La enfermedad es una dolencia,
las discusiones familiares
son una dolencia, el caos social
es una dolencia.

想要家庭吉祥、和睦，
就應該常常起歡喜心，
天天為自己的家庭祝福。

To have a warm and happy family,
we should nurture a heart of joy
and shower our family with blessings.

家族の吉祥と和睦を願うなら、
常に歓喜の心をもって毎日自分の家族の
ため祝福すべきである。

Para disfrutar de una
vida familiar cálida y feliz,
debemos nutrir el corazón
con alegría y colmar
a nuestra familia de bendiciones.

勇氣不可失，信心不可無，
世間沒有不能與無能的事，
只怕——不肯。

Never lose courage.
Never lose faith.
Nothing in this world is impossible
when you are determined.

勇気と自信を失ってはならない。
やる気さえあれば、
この世にはやれない事も
できない事もないはず。
やらないだけなのだ。

Nunca pierdas el coraje.
Nunca pierdas la fe.
Nada en este mundo es imposible
cuando tienes determinación.

不管路有多遠、自己的能力有多少，
都能隨分隨力盡量去達成目標，
此即「毅力」。

Regardless how far the
journey is or how capable we are,
we do our best to reach our goal.
This is perseverance at its best.

どんなに道が遠かろうと、
また己の能力がどれ程であろうと、
それ相応にベストを尽くして目標を達成する。
これがすなわち「剛毅さ」である。

Sin importar cuán largo es el camino o
cuán capaces somos, hacemos lo
mejor posible para alcanzar nuestra meta.
Esta es la mejor muestra de perseverancia.

苦幹象徵毅力和耐力，
要成就大業，
必須擁有苦幹的精神。

Hardwork signifies
persistence and patience.
To achieve
great accomplishments, we must have a
hardworking spirit.

一生懸命さは剛毅さと忍耐力の象徴である。
大業を成就するにはこの精神を
持たなければならない。

El trabajar duro significa
persistencia y paciencia.
Para alcanzar grandes logros
debemos poseer un espíritu luchador.

有力量去愛人
或被愛的人，都是幸福的人。

True blessings flow from our ability to love,
and be loved by others.

人を愛せる人も、
また愛される人も、みな幸せな人である。

Las personas felices son aquellas
que tienen capacidad
para amar y ser amados.

要培養一分清淨無染的愛。
在感情上不要有得失心，
不要想回收，就不會有煩惱。

Learn to develop pure and
unconditional love;
a love that has no sense of gain or loss,
that asks for nothing in return.
In this way we can be free of worries.

清浄無垢の愛を培うには、
損得を無視し、
見返りを求めないことである。
そうすれば煩悩はない。

Aprende a desarrollar un amor
puro e incondicional, un amor
que no sabe del perder o ganar,
que no pide nada a cambio.
De esta forma podemos
liberarnos de las preocupaciones.

222

有所求的愛，是無法永久存在的。
能夠永久存在的，
是那分無形、無染且無求的愛。

A love with conditions
attached would never last.
Only pure, unconditional love
will last forever.

見返りを求める愛は長続きしない。
永久に保つことができるのは、
形なく、汚れなくそして見返りを
求めない愛である。

El amor con condiciones
nunca perdurará.
Sólo el amor puro e incondicional
vivirá para siempre.

愛要濃淡合宜，像清茶淡香；
若是太濃，則苦得喝不下。

Love is just like a cup of tea;
when properly mixed,
it has a wonderful light aroma.
If it is too strong,
it will be too bitter to drink.

愛は濃すぎず薄すぎず。

お茶は芳しく、美味しく、また気を引き立てる。

だが、濃すぎると苦くて飲めなくなる。

世間の愛もこれと同じである。

El amor es como una taza de té,
sabe delicioso y tiene un aroma suave cuando
se mezcla apropiadamente.
Si es muy fuerte, será demasiado amargo
para poder tomarlo.

任何事都是從一個決心、
一粒種子開始。

Every achievement grows out of
the seed of determination.

何事も決意することから始まる。
一粒の種から成長するのだ。

Cada logro germina de la semilla
de la determinación.

不要小看自己，
因為人有無限的可能。

Don't underestimate yourself,
for human beings have unlimited potential.

自分自身を過小評価することはない。
人はだれしも無限の可能性を
潜めているのだから。

No subestimes tu capacidad,
todos tenemos un potencial ilimitado.

千里之路，必須從第一步開始；
聖人的境域，也是自凡夫起步。

The journey of a thousand miles
begins with one first step.
Even the saint was once
an ordinary human being.

千里の道も始めの一歩から踏み出すのだ。
たとえ聖人の境地に到達した人といえども、
凡人として第一歩から始めたのだ。

El viaje de las mil millas
empieza con el primer paso.
Aún el santo fue una vez un ser humano
como cualquier otro.

發心容易，恆心難持；
光說不練，無法體悟真理，
實踐道法。

To begin is easy, to persist, difficult.
Talking about truth without practicing it
leads neither to enlightenment
nor realizing the Dharma.

発心することは簡単だが、
常に変わらない心を持続することは
容易ではない。
言うだけで行わないなら、
真理を悟ることができず、
み仏の道を実践することはできない。

Comenzar es fácil, persistir es difícil.
Hablar sobre la verdad sin practicarla no
lleva al entendimiento ni al Dharma.

人生在世，不能無所事事、
懵懵懂懂而虛度一生，
應發揮我們的良知良能，
造福人群。

We should not idle away our time,
and drift in frivolous thoughts.
It is best to nurture our innate goodness
and develop our ability to help others.

生きているからには、
何もせずにぼんやりと過ごして
一生を棒に振ってしまわないようにしよう。
それには良知良能を発揮し、
人々に幸せをもたらすべきである。

*No debemos desperdiciar
nuestro tiempo y desviarnos
con pensamientos frívolos.
Es mejor nutrir nuestra bondad innata
y desarrollar nuestra capacidad
para ayudar a los demás.*

人一旦無所事事、虛度光陰，
　　精神就會萎靡不振，
　　生命也就失去意義。

When we have nothing to do
and idle away our time,
our spirit becomes weak
and life seems meaningless.

何もすることなく、
ぶらぶらと時間を無駄にしていると、
精神は衰えて振るわなくなり
生命の意義を失う。

Cuando no tenemos nada
que hacer y desperdiciamos
nuestro tiempo, el espíritu
se vuelve débil y la vida no tiene sentido.

美滿的人生，
不在物質、權勢、名利及地位，
而在人與人之間的關愛與情誼。

A fulfilling life is not preoccupied
with material objects, prestige, or power.
It is a life that is filled with true friendships,
sharing, and caring for each other.

幸せな人生は
物質、権勢、名利、地位によるのではなく、
人間同士の互いの思いやりによるのであり、
良いつながりをもつことによる。

Una vida plena no consiste en tener
más objetos materiales,
más prestigio o más poder.
Una vida plena se llena
con amistades verdaderas,
el compartir y el cuidarnos mutuamente.

所謂看開人生，
不是悲觀，而是積極樂觀；
不是看破，而是看透。

To not take things in life so seriously
is not a negative, resigned attitude;
it is a happy and proactive one.
It does not mean giving up hope;
it is a genuine insight
into the real purpose of life.

人生を達観するということは悲観ではなく、
むしろ積極的で楽観的な態度である。
諦めではなく見極めである。

Tomar la vida no tan seriamente,
no es una actitud negativa ni resignada.
Es buena y proactiva.
No significa perder la esperanza,
es la comprensión verdadera
del propósito real de la vida.

所謂看開人生，
並非什麼都不做，
而是能及時行善；
也不是什麼都沒有，
而是什麼都知足！

To not take things in life so seriously
does not mean being indifferent;
rather, it implies the attitude of
grasping every opportunity to do good.
It does not mean not owning anything,
but being content
with whatever you have.

人生を達観するということは
何もしないのではなく、
時を移さずに善を行うのである。
達観して何一つ持たないのではなく、
何一つ不足しないのである。

243

Tomar la vida sin preocupaciones
no significa no hacer nada, sino aprovechar
cualquier oportunidad
para hacer buenas obras.
No significa no tener nada,
sino estar feliz con lo que se tiene.

人生幾十年的成就，
都是由每一天的言行累積而成。
所以，要照顧好每一天的言行。

Our accomplishments in life
are built on the words and actions
we make every day —
thus we must be discreet in our
daily speech and behavior.

人生数十年の成就は、
日々の言行の積み重ねによって成る。
よって、日々の言行に
気をつけなければならない。

Los logros en nuestras vidas
se construyen con las palabras y
las acciones de cada día.
Por eso, sé discreto en lo que dices y
en tu comportamiento diario.

246

能施與的人，
比受施的人更有福。

To give is better than
to receive.

施すことは施しを受けるより幸せである。

Dar es mejor que recibir.

真正的布施，
除了無欲無求，
還要有感恩心。

Give without expectation,
and give with gratitude.

真正なる布施は無償であるほか、
感謝の気持ちがなければならない。

Da sin esperar nada a cambio,
y da con gratitud.

250

布施不是有錢人的專利，
而是一分虔誠的愛心。

Giving is not the privilege of the rich,
it is the privilege of the sincere.

布施は富める者に与えられた特許ではない。

それは誰にもできる、

誠意のこもった愛の心づくしである。

El dar no es privilegio de los ricos,
es el privilegio de las personas sinceras.

靜思語

靜思語 Jing Si Aphorisms 一
中文、English、日本語、Español 典藏版

著　作　者	釋證嚴
英 文 翻 譯	美國、馬來西亞慈濟英文翻譯志工
英文最後編輯	陳素羚、石欣芳 (感謝 Douglas Shaw 和美國慈濟翻譯小組)
英文協助編輯	Neil Bond
西班牙文翻譯	慈濟西班牙語翻譯小組
西班牙文校閱	王振國
日 文 翻 譯	涂羅美麗
日 文 校 閱	山田智美
策　　　劃	徐秀華、林幸惠
責 任 編 輯	高秋絨、杜晴惠
美 術 設 計	王順瑜
封 面 設 計	王慧莉
出 版 者	慈濟文化出版社
地　　　址	臺北市忠孝東路三段217巷7弄19號
電　　　話	(02)2898-9888
傳　　　真	(02)2898-9889
郵 撥 帳 號	06677883互愛文化志業股份有限公司
印 製 者	新豪華製版印刷股份有限公司
出 版 日	2005年 8月初版(5000本)
	2013年 3月再版一刷
	行政院新聞局局版臺業字第4934號
定　　　價	178元

ISBN：978-986-5919-03-0（平裝）

Printed in Taiwan

國家圖書館出版品預行編目資料

靜思語 = Jing Si Aphorisms/ 釋證嚴著. --
再版. -- 臺北市 : 慈濟文化, 2013.03 [民102]
256面 ; 13 x18公分
典藏版 中英日西對照
ISBN 978-986-5919-03-0(平裝)

1.佛教說法 2.佛教教化法

225.4　　　　　　　　　　102004835

Jing Si Aphorisms

Jing Si Aphorisms—
中文、*English*、日本語、*Español*

Author: *Shih Cheng Yen*

English translation by: *U.S. and Malaysia Tzu Chi translation volunteers*

English final editors: *Sulian Chen and Lissa Shih, with special thanks to Douglas Shaw and U.S. Tzu Chi Translation Team*

English contributing editor: *Neil Bond*

Las Traductoras Españolas: *Equipo de Traducción Española del Tzu Chi*

El Revisor Español: *Francisco Wang*

和　　訳：涂羅美麗、三宅教子

日本語校閲：山田智美

Planning: *Theresa Hsu, Lin Hsin-huei*

Managing editors: *Teresa Kao, Sunny Duh*

Art editors: *Cecilia Wang*

Cover design: *Wang Huei-li*

Publisher: *Tzu Chi Cultural Publishing Co.*

Address：*No.19, Alley 7, Lane 217, Sec.3, Zhongxiao East Rd., Taipei, Taiwan.*

Tel: *886-2-2898-9888*

Fax: *886-2-2898-9889*

http://www.jingsi.com.tw/

Printed in Taiwan
ISBN：*978-986-5919-03-0*

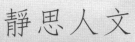

静思人文

JING SI PUBLICATIONS *http://www.jingsi.com.tw/*